I Need a Knee Replacement, Now What?

(How to Prepare for Knee Replacement Surgery)

Kimberly Dixon, M.Ed., CPC, CCRC

ISBN:152365046x
ISBN-13:9781523650460

DEDICATION

I dedicate this book to my sister Valerie. Thank you for traveling with me on my hospital tour (inside joke). You were with me every step of the way. The love, support and care you show me is unparalleled. I am grateful to have you as my physical and spiritual sister.

CONTENTS

ACKNOWLEDGMENTS

Thank you to my parents, Sharon Simmons and Samuel Dixon, for your love and support.

A special thank you to my best friend Kesha for being my private duty nurse after both my total knee replacement surgeries, and for being one of my biggest cheerleaders.

Thank you to my brother Malcolm and Mr. Sutton, for walking me through the knee replacement process. Your advice was invaluable. Thank you to my spiritual mentor Rev. Angel Onley-Livingston, who kept saying, "Write the book!"

Lastly and most importantly, I want to thank God for his covering and protection and for providing a refuge for me when I felt I could not go on. It is only because of Him that I made it!

FOREWARD

"God, who is this beautiful being of light?" These were the words I spoke to God, when Kimberly came bursting through the door in joy and light at my women's retreat. Kimberly began to speak and share her experience, about being ready to change your life as the most important step. I sat back in my chair in our beach home for the weekend and gave Kimberly the floor to teach as I listened and learned. Kimberly taught what she learned about life and gave us what she had been given from God! Kimberly's presence in this book is the same as if seeing her in the physical. Kimberly's joy, humor, and straight to the point voice in this self-help booklet will be life transforming for anyone who is considering or who needs knee replacement. Kimberly has a way of teaching you and encouraging you through just mere conversation. The conversation in this book is clear and motivating!

Over the past 15 years, many of my family members have had knee replacements, and I am all too aware of what it means to be the person on the sideline watching the process of decisions, recovery, and healing. I wish as a counselor and spiritual/pastoral counselor that I'd had this book earlier *I Need a Knee Replacement, Now What?* to give to my family members. In this book, she talks about making choices, being informed, being prepared, and going through the surgery. This reminded me of books I read as I wrote my birth plan to give to my OBGYN for how I wanted my birthing process to go. This book is truly a Knee Replacement Plan!

Coach Kimberly has a way of using her coaching skills to nudge you along to deal with the reality of what is needed for you to go forward in any goal or need, and to push your way through until the end result is reached. Kimberly is my personal life coach and as a National Board Certified Counselor, I understand the need for everyone to have someone to help them along the way. In coaching, Kimberly leaves no room for giving up, but every option to win in this process called life!

This book will be instrumental in the coming years to medical professionals as a tool to pass on to their patients as a way to help encourage them through the process of having this procedure. I believe this book will begin to solidify the need for life coaches and/or counselors with a background and or experience of the symptoms and or diagnosis; who are living a healthy, healed lifestyle to be present and available in the offices of practitioners everywhere. This book will continuously help to give you as the patient considering knee replacement, a listening, encouraging ear that is dedicated to listening and helping the patient go from diagnosis of symptoms and treatment planning, to understanding that someone is right there to guide you along in the process.

Rev. Angel Onley-Livingston, NBCC, LPC
House of Abba Family Outreach Center LLC
Author of *Healing While Grieving*

INTRODUCTION

As each has received a gift, employ it in serving one another, as good managers of the grace of God in its various forms.
- 1 Peter 4:10

My Background

My orthopedist said,

Your anterior cruciate ligament (ACL) is torn to shreds. "Ok, God, what do you want me to learn?"

Your arthritis spread to the entire knee. "Ok, God what do you want me to learn?"

You need a cane to walk. "Ok, God what do want me to learn?"

You need a leg brace to walk. "Ok, God how can I use this to help someone else?"

With every new obstacle, I asked the question.

Questioning helped end my suffering by opening my heart. It ended my life time of suffering because I clearly understood that my bow legs were not about me. My journey was about giving me the tools I need to help other chronic pain suffers. Had I not gone through everything I experienced from age 4 to 45, I simply would not have the knowledge needed for this assignment. My life is a lesson for others.

What I viewed as a curse, became my biggest blessing. Through my journey with bow legs, arthritis and many surgeries, I gained a deeper spiritual relationship with God and I learned how to recognize pain in others. I know how a person in pain moves, I recognize the deep sadness in their eyes. This discernment allowed me to have many interactions with people of every walk in every place imaginable.

On November 10, 1970, I entered this world as a bubbly, happy baby. I am now happy and bubbly again. The road to get back to this state was one heck of a journey.

When I was born, I was extremely bow-legged. As a result, I had difficulty learning to walk. Ok, that is an understatement. That I could not walk is the truth. Every time I took a step, I fell. The inability to walk led to my first surgery on both legs at four years old. That was the first of many surgeries.

After each surgery, my legs eventually bowed back out. That caused an uneven pressure on my knees. That pressure led to me being diagnosed with arthritis in both knees at 12 years old. My teenage years were marred by physical pain. While other teenage girls day-dreamed about boys and going to the mall, my mind focused on how badly my knees hurt. I never told anyone how much pain I was in. I suffered in silence.

I managed to get through my teen years and 20s without any surgeries. My 30s were a different story entirely. In 2003, I had an arthroscopic surgery to repair what the surgeon thought was a simple cartilage tear in my right knee. The surgeon was horrified at what he found. The arthritis damage was so severe that I had spots with no cartilage at all. The bone friction led to the base of my femur bleeding into my joint. The surgeon was stunned that I was still able to walk on my right leg at all. The doctor told me that my knee needed replacement, but I was too young. I was 32 years old. (Medical recommendation and technology at that time did not support knee replacement at such a young age).

By my late 30s, I experienced excruciating pain on a daily basis. I could barely walk. Standing for more than a few minutes made my knees burn like they were on fire. On a daily basis I pushed myself to take another step. I was mentally and physically tired. Years later, I realized that I experienced a spiritual crisis as well. I knew who God was but I felt forgotten.

Sitting on my couch one day, I had a screaming, crying conversation with God. You see, I always knew that I was destined to be a teacher. I had a vision of teaching when I was 25 years. On the day of the crying, screaming fit, I was on the verge of completing my masters degree in education. I had no idea what to do once completed because I knew that I could never teach on a college campus. I could not walk across my living room, so hiking across a huge campus every day or even a few days a week, was out of the question.

God's response to me was, "I never said you were a college professor." That revelation blew me out of the water. I was confused. If I am not a college professor then what kind of teacher am I? This prompted me to ask more questions of God. With each new situation I began asking, "What do you want me to learn from this?" Through asking that question, I learned that I was to teach others based on my life experiences.

Throughout my entire childhood, I thought that my bow-legs were a punishment for some unknown crime. I spent many days hiding the profound sadness that hung over my head like a dark rain cloud. The weight of carrying that secret slowly ate away at my soul. I knew that I was not intended to suffer that way. That crying, screaming fit was my surrender to God's purpose for my life. That crying, screaming fit saved my life.

That day I started my mission to learn as much as I could about bow legs and arthritis. More importantly, I began to view each new challenge I faced as an opportunity to learn. And learn, I did!

In 2003, I learned that I needed my right knee to be replaced. In 2011, I learned that what I considered to be my good knee, my left knee was shot, too. In 2015, 12 years after learning that I needed a knee replacement, I finally got my knees replaced. As I write this book, I sit on the couch with my leg elevated after having my 3rd surgery this year. On March 24, 2015, I had right total knee replacement. On April 4, 2015, I had right knee incision revision surgery. My knee stopped healing around day 10, and surgery removed the fluid in it. There was no infection, thank God! On December 29, 2015, I had left total knee replacement.

I spent most of the year recovering from surgery and rehabbing my knee. I entered 2016 still rehabbing my knee. Physical therapy continues 8-12 weeks after surgery. Yet 2015 was one of the best years of my life. 2015 was the year I started to live again. After years of waiting to get my knees replaced, my dream came true. 2016 brings so many opportunities. I am full of anticipation.

My mission now is to help others as they go through the journey of degenerative arthritis and knee replacement surgery.

These pages share some of what I learned from my many surgeries and multiple stints in physical therapy.

This book is a guide. It is short and simple by design. My philosophy in life is to keep it simple. Total knee replacement surgery requires planning. Many people won't have the time or the desire to read a 200 page guide in the weeks prior to surgery. So here it is short and sweet, and most importantly, simple!

Why You Need a Knee Replacement

The knee connects the thigh bone (femur) to the shin (tibia). It works as a hinge that allows walking, side to side movement as well as standing. The bone is covered by cartilage. Cartilage is a thin, smooth, rubbery tissue that allows the bones to glide smoothly over each other. The meniscus cartilage acts as a shock absorber.

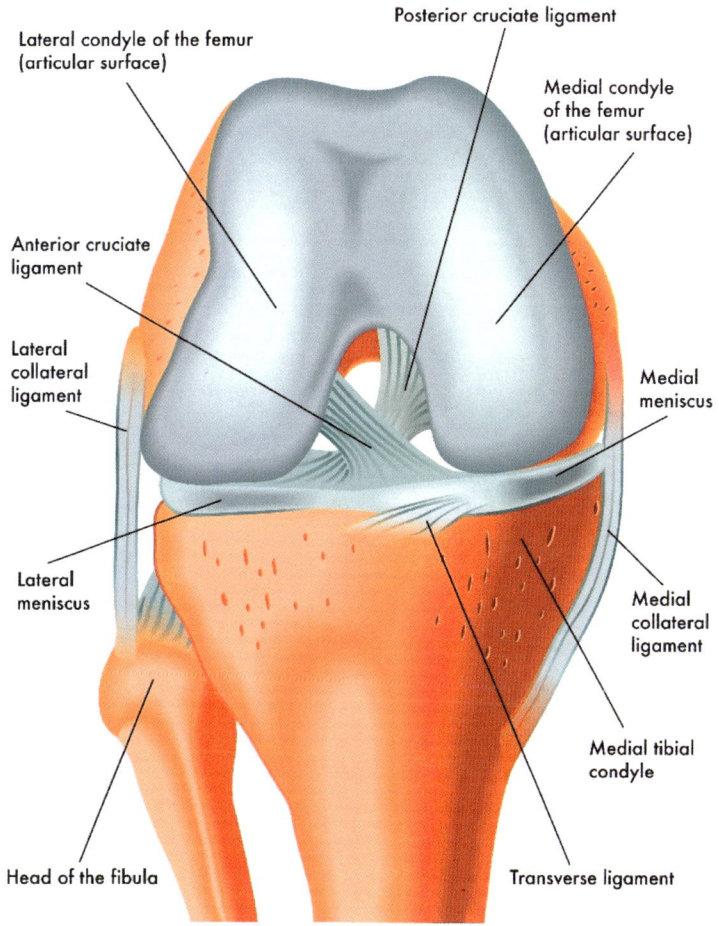

Bone, cartilage, ligaments, tendons and muscles all work together in a healthy joint.

Knee replacement becomes necessary when the joint no longer functions properly due to natural wear and tear, injury, arthritis, diseases such as rheumatoid arthritis and gout, or other conditions that put unnatural stress on the knee. As the cartilage becomes more damaged and worn, the ends of the bone become exposed. Bones now rub against each other.

The misalignment of bow legs and knock knees are two conditions that put unnatural stress on the joint. That unnatural stress often leads to osteoarthritis, the most common form of arthritis.

Arthritis is characterized by pain that is mild to excruciating. It may be a dull pain, a sharp pain, or pain that comes and goes. As arthritis in the joint worsens, so does the pain. Pain is often accompanied by swelling and tenderness, snapping and crackling noises with movement, giving way, and locking.

STAGE OF KNEE OSTEOARTHRITIS

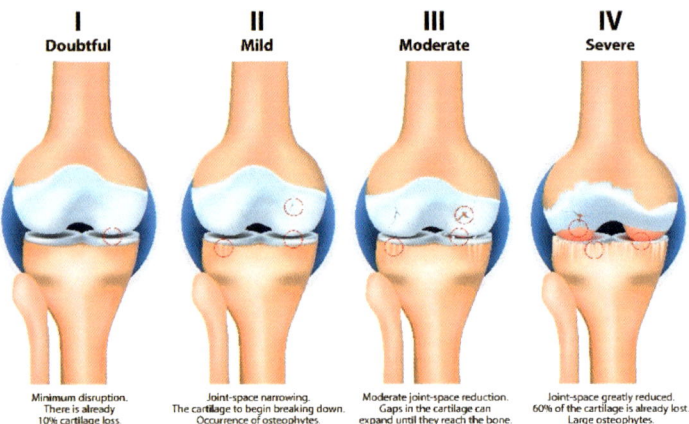

I	II	III	IV
Doubtful	**Mild**	**Moderate**	**Severe**

Minimum disruption. There is already 10% cartilage loss.

Joint-space narrowing. The cartilage to begin breaking down. Occurrence of osteophytes.

Moderate joint-space reduction. Gaps in the cartilage can expand until they reach the bone.

Joint-space greatly reduced. 60% of the cartilage is already lost. Large osteophytes.

Knee replacement is not the first option used to treat joint disorders and pain. (See my book *I Have Arthritis: Now What?* for more treatment options). Knee replacement becomes necessary when the pain interferes with your quality of life, your ability to move the knee is reduced due to severe pain, stiffness and swelling, you are unable to perform everyday tasks such as getting out of the bathtub or shopping, you no longer have a normal social life or can no longer work or you become depressed because of the ongoing pain and lack of mobility.

**This is a very high overview of the knee and knee problems. I am not a medical professional. As such, I am not offering medical advice. This booklet provides information from a patient's perspective, and attempts to make scientific medical information more easily understandable.

Kimberly Dixon, M.Ed., CPC, CCRC

CHAPTER ONE
CHOICES

Every new day is another chance to change your life.
- Native American Proverb

Is knee replacement surgery an obstacle or an opportunity? The choice is yours. Every situation in life offers a choice. Which choice you make is your decision. Even in situations where all the options are rotten, the choice is still yours. Knee replacement surgery is no different. You have a choice. Make a decision today and stand by your choice.

Is knee replacement the worse thing ever, or is it an opportunity to get your life back?

Is it the most horrific thing you ever encountered, or is it an opportunity to walk with less pain?

Record your answer here:

_____

_____

_____

If you choose it as the worst thing ever, then stop reading now because this book is not for you. The focus of this book is to show you how to approach knee replacement surgery with a positive attitude, and to help you get prepared. The surgery is not a walk in the park. Your attitude about the surgery has a huge impact on the outcome of the surgery. Whatever you choose, you get. The choice is yours.

If you decide knee replacement surgery is the worst thing that could ever happen, it will be the worst thing that ever happens. Your mind is your most powerful tool. You can use it to empower and uplift you, or you can use it to create a self-fulfilling prophecy in which you lose.

Decide today to approach knee replacement surgery as an opportunity.

In addition to your attitude, you must be careful about who you listen to. You get many unsolicited opinions from well-intended friends and family. Unfortunately, rarely do they share stories of triumph and joy. What they share most often are horror stories that they heard through the rumor mill.

The story goes something like this.

Well-intended friend: "Ohhhhh, I'm so sorry you need surgery. You know my neighbor's, sister's, cousin from Oakland, you know the one married to Bob had the same surgery. Her knee was never right after that. I don't know what happened or what went wrong but my neighbor told me she is just in pain every day now. Poor thing is just miserable. I hope you have a good surgeon. What's your doctor's name?"

You: "Dr. XYZ"

Well-intended friend: "I never heard of him. Are you sure he is any good? I hope he is for your sake."

Are you kidding me! I am facing a major surgery and this is how you encourage me? Nobody wants or needs to hear that! I am not sure what makes people share such stories, but get prepared, because they will. Again, you have a choice. You can listen to the rumor mill or make the best decision for you based on your own circumstances.

Whenever someone attempts to share a horror story about someone else, simply inform them that you are sorry they had poor results, but that you believe that it won't be your story. On the other hand, I believe it is alright to listen to a firsthand story. You may gain valuable insight into what you should and shouldn't do.

For example, after my right knee replacement, my surgeon and all the hospital discharge instructions explicitly said that I should not get the incision wet. However the home health nurse said in her opinion that it was okay for me to take showers but not to use soap on the incision. I chose to follow the home nurse opinion because I wanted to take a shower. Shortly after starting daily showers, my incision stopped healing. As a result I had an incision revision surgery exactly 2 weeks after my TKR surgery. I firmly believe that municipal water and all it contains caused my incision to stop healing. After my left knee placement surgery, I still took showers but made sure to cover the incision with plastic wrap and tape. The incision stayed perfectly dry and it healed completely.

This story is my first-hand account. I had knee replacement surgery and this is my story. It contains insight into how to care for your incision and it is an example of what happens when you choose not to follow doctor's orders.

Sadly enough, people knowingly and unknowingly pass along stories with little to no accuracy. Important details like the person with the bad result never followed the PT regime. They did not start a daily walking routine or follow any other instructions. Granted some people do have complications after surgery, joint replacement is a major surgery and it carries risks just as every other surgery.

To get good results (less pain and more mobility) after joint replacement, you must put in the work. Some days are good. Some days are bad. However, you have to work every day to regain function and mobility.

We all have gremlins in our head and it is best not to feed them. Listening to horror stories and the rumor mill allows the gremlins to take control. Once they control your thoughts and actions, you will head down the "what if" path. You start to imagine all sorts of horrific scenarios in which the outcome is always tragic and sad. Have you ever asked yourself a "what if" question and the results were positive? It rarely ever happens. "What ifs" spread terror and panic. More importantly, they prolong your suffering. By playing "what if" scenarios in your head, you talk yourself out of a surgery which you desperately need. You hobble along in serious pain years longer than you need to because you let the gremlins run free.

Online videos are another way we feed gremlins. If watching a live surgery is too much for you to handle now, do NOT watch a knee replacement surgery online before you have surgery! It is tempting because you want to know exactly what the doctor will do. Knee replacement surgery is graphic and requires major changes to attach the artificial knee. It is a lot to take in.

I love medical information and surgeries, so I decided after having my right knee replaced but before getting the left one done that I wanted to watch an actual surgery. I swiftly stopped that video. A few seconds into it, I knew that I would not go through with my surgery if I watched that video. It was too much to handle. Watching that video was an open invitation to let the gremlins run free. Do yourself a huge favor and keep them in a box with the lid on it!

Make a choice now, don't listen to the rumor mill, put in the work every day, and do not let the gremlins in your head out of the box.

CHAPTER TWO
BE INFORMED

That the wise man may hear, and increase in learning; that the man of understanding may attain to sound counsel.
- Proverbs 1:5

No one knows you better than you. This is true whether or not you face an upcoming knee replacement surgery.

However, that statement is only true if you know your body and are connected to it. Self-awareness means you know how your body feels and how it responds and reacts to changes. You are connected and in tune to you. That connection allows you to instinctively know when something is not right with you mentally, physically and spiritually. You feel it in your gut, you feel in your bones. You just know.

Personally, I know when I am about to get an infection long before I get one. Oddly, I can smell it and taste it. Weird, right? But I can. The first time I had an upper respiratory infection, I went to my primary care physician before I had full blown symptoms. He asked why I thought I was sick. I didn't have a fever and I didn't look sick. I told him I smelled it and tasted it. He laughed and sent me home without any medication. Two days later, I visited him again. I looked very different and had all the indication of an upper respiratory infection. He was stunned. I don't think this is a special talent or gift I have. I think we all have this ability when we pay attention to our own bodies.

Listen to your body. What is it telling you?

In my twenties, I was on a mission to make sure I didn't become a diabetic or develop high blood pressure. Both are prevalent in my family and I didn't want that for myself. As a result, I used to check in with myself to see how I felt. This slightly odd behavior helped me tap into me. So I know when I don't feel "right" long before I get sick. When I did become pre-hypertensive in my late 30's I knew something was wrong. Typically, people don't notice such a minor change in blood pressure, but I did.

My doctor learned that I knew me. Now let me say, he did not dispense pills when I was not sick but he always listened to my concerns and helped me avoid sickness. By the way, it is my personal opinion that if you have a doctor who gives you medicine simply because you asked for it, he/she is not a good doctor and you need to leave that doctor. They are the medical professionals with the medical training. They should always listen to you and address your concerns but not be your personal dispensary. Medication should not be handed out because you saw the commercial and know that you have "it". Whatever "it" is. That's just my opinion.

Knowing yourself also means knowing your numbers, blood pressure, glucose, cholesterol, etc. I am always stunned and honestly a little sad when people don't bother to know information about themselves.

How do you know if your blood pressure is running a little high lately if you don't know what it normally is? The answer is, you don't. We rely on doctors to keep us healthy but that is our job. Doctors treat us when we are sick.

My blood pressure was low after both total knee replacements which is not uncommon. The nurse asked me what my blood pressure normally is. I told her. She smiled and said, "You would be surprised at the number of people who don't know their blood pressure." Based on the information I provided she determined that it was low but not much lower than it normally is, I am no longer pre-hypertensive.

Know your medications or keep a list of them with you at all times.

The day of surgery and throughout your hospital stay, you are repeatedly asked your name, date of birth, medications, surgery type and surgery location (left or right). Don't get mad at the questions. As irritating as it is to repeatedly answer the same question, keep your cool. These questions are designed to keep you safe. Answer them truthfully. That is not the time to make jokes or omit information! Your life literally depends on it.

Medication List

Medication	Dosage	Frequency

CHAPTER THREE
GET PREPARED

You can't stop the waves, but you can learn to surf.
- Hawaiian Proverb

Preparing for surgery or any leave of absence from work requires coordination between you, your physician, the employer, your employer and your health insurance company. Preparation ensures that everything goes as smoothly as possible, and that all the moving parts are coordinated.

I remember the first surgery I had as an adult. I did not know exactly what I needed to do. I did not know what Family and Medical Leave Act (FMLA), short-term disability or long-term disability were. The weeks after my surgery were spent fielding phone calls instead of resting and recovering. Handling disability claim problems or insurance problems is somewhat difficult. It is even more difficult when you are on painkillers.

Get prepared before your surgery to reduce the likelihood of encountering problems.

Let's begin with a few definitions.

FMLA – Family and Medical Leave Act – entitles employees in the United States (U.S.) to take 12 weeks of unpaid leave in a 12-month period. FMLA calculates on a 12 month period, not a traditional calendar year. This is a Federal law.

FMLA covers:
1. Birth of a child.

2. Adoption or fostering a new child.

3. A serious health condition for the employee, spouse, child, or parent of the employee.

4. Any qualifying exigency that arises from the above when a spouse, child, or parent is an active military.

5. 26 weeks of leave is available to care for a covered service member with a serious injury under military caregiver leave.

Once the 12 weeks are exhausted, your job protection ends. That essentially means your employer now can determine to keep you as an employee or end your employment.

Short-term disability – A medical disability lasting more than 14 days but less than 180 days.

Long-term disability – A medical disability lasting more than 180 calendar days.

Short-term and long-term disability insurance – When offered by an employer, they allow an employee to receive pay while out of work. The amount is typically a percentage of the employee's regular salary. The percentage range is based on the individual employer's employee benefits.

**Short-term and long-term disability insurance (also known as medical gap insurance) are available for purchase individually. Be sure to read the exclusions. A few years ago, I wanted to buy a policy outside of what my employer offers, and every company I contacted wanted to exclude any and all knee or leg surgery. In my case purchasing an extra, outside short-term disability insurance policy was not in my best interests because of the policy exclusions.

Step 1

After setting my surgery date with my physician, the first call I made was to my employer's disability claim handler to report my FMLA covered absence and start my disability leave claim (so that I got paid while out of work). My employer uses an outside contractor to handle leaves of absence; however, some organizations handle it in-house. If you are unsure how your employer handles leaves of absence, contact your human resources department. Failing to complete this step may result in the delay of short-term leave benefits or the denial of benefits (ouch!).

In emergency situations contact your disability department as soon as possible.

My next call was to my director. You do not need to disclose the exact reason for your medical leave, however you do need to tell them of your upcoming absence from work. As a courtesy I also e-mailed my peers at work. I chose to do so because I work closely with my peers and they are aware of my ongoing knee problems and many of them are my personal friends.

After a few days, I contacted my health insurance company to verify that my doctor's office got authorization for my surgery. Many health insurance companies require approval for surgery and inpatient hospital stays. If the admission is not pre-authorized, the PATIENT accesses a fee for not getting the hospital stay pre-certified. Although the doctor's office completes this step, it is the patient's responsibility to make sure it is complete before being admitted.

Overview:

1. Report your leave absence to your disability leave department. This may be an outside contractor, your employee health department or human resources. **Complete ALL forms sent to you and return them to the correct department.

2. Inform your manager or team-lead of your absence.

3. After a few days, contact your health insurance carrier to make sure that any pre-admission certification or approvals are on file.

4. Make follow-up calls if any of the above steps are not complete.

Following a few simple steps before surgery or any leave of absence makes the process simpler and easier.

*This information applies only to the U.S. Outside of the U.S. follow the regulations and insurance guidelines for your country or region.

Step 2

This step of TKR surgery actually began long before setting the actual surgery date. This step involves preparing financially for the surgery.

I started preparing for the financial impact of total knee replacement 2 years before I actually had the surgery. Surgery is costly. At a time when you have the least income, you will have more expenses than usual. Every year many bankruptcies are the direct result of overwhelming medical expenses. The cost and financial implications of surgery are multi-faceted.

First, there is the cost of the surgery which includes a separate bill from the surgeon, assistant surgeon, hospital and the anesthesiologist.

Then there is the cost for any post-operative care such as physical therapy (PT), occupational therapy (OT) and home health visits (weekly nurse visits to monitor progress and check for signs of complications). Generally, after an arthroscopy surgery you can expect to have PT 2-3 times per week from 4-12 weeks depending on the type of surgery, your physical health, and your age.

PT for my ACL Reconstruction surgery in 2010 lasted 16 weeks. My general health is good but my recovery was extremely slow. The surgery replaced my badly damaged ACL but did not correct the arthritis damage and I was 40. As we age, we heal more slowly. Trying to rebuild strength and flexibility with arthritis in both knees was not easy, but I did it. Setting aside funds for PT ensures that you can actually afford to go to PT. The last thing you want is to need more PT, but not be able to afford it. Missing PT puts you at risk of not regaining full function.

Although I saved for the surgery, I still was not prepared. I was out of work 6 weeks instead of the two I was initially told, and PT dragged on for months. I almost lost everything. My car was in danger of repossession. I borrowed from Peter to pay Paul. It was a horrible experience. It was difficult to focus on healing with all the financial pressure looming over my head. I was sad because nothing seemed to go as planned. I was scared because my financial resources were dried up. I had nothing left and nowhere to turn. Just as I reached the end of the rope, I went back to work. It took years to recover from that financial debacle.

Lastly, you must factor in your monthly living expenses such as mortgage or rent, utilities, car payments, credit card payments, and groceries. Every expense you typically have on a month-to-month basis continues. If you have disability coverage through your mortgage, credit cards, and the like, follow each company's guidelines for filing a claim. Not following each companies guidelines exactly may cause denial of your claim.

Financial preparation includes:

1. Putting extra money in savings each month. When you have ongoing medical issues, saving is difficult but it is not impossible. Setting aside small amounts adds up over time.

2. Setting money aside in a flexible spending account (FSA). Most companies offer an FSA as part of their employer benefits. If you plan your surgery in advance, you have the option to set aside pre-tax dollars to cover the cost of the medical bills. Most hospitals require the patient to pay their deductible and coinsurance at check-in the day of surgery. FSA funds are an excellent way to cover these expenses.

3. Stockpiling non-perishable food and household supplies. By using coupons I created a sizeable stockpile of non-perishable food, household supplies and personal care items. While on work disability leave, you will not have to buy any of these items.

4. If you have student loans, applying for forbearance while you are out of work temporarily stops your student loan payment.

5. Paying off as many credit card or other small bills as possible.

Preparing for the financial implications of surgery requires hard work but is achievable with careful planning.

Step 3

This step is not a physical step you take; it is a psychological one. When we think of who we are we often think of our name, professional titles and the roles we play in life such as mother. It is only natural that we think of our physical bodies as "who" we are. The truth is; you are simply a spiritual being.

In a recent conversation with a coaching client, we discussed her upcoming hip replacement surgery. She stated that although she needed and wanted the hip replacement, she felt an internal resistance to actually replacing "her" hip with an artificial joint.

I knew exactly what she was referring to, as it was the same resistance or reluctance I felt towards parting with my knees. After all the years of pain, I still had a churning feeling in my stomach which I could not put my finger on. What was this feeling? What was this really about? I was happy. I was excited. I was full of anticipation. I was reluctant.

The realization about this step was not one I sat down and thought about, although I felt it. I took this step quite unexpectedly sitting in a hot bath two weeks before my right total knee replacement.

As I sat in the bath, I thought about my life and all I went through as a result of arthritis. I began to say a prayer of thanks to God. Without his protection, covering and love I would not have made it.

What happened next shocked me. I began to gently rub my knee and thank it for supporting me all these years. I thanked it for continuing to work even though it was badly damaged, I thanked it for never letting me down, as it buckled many times but I never fell. When I did fall, it was because I tripped over my own feet or something I left in the floor! I thanked it for working when it shouldn't have. For every surgery I had as an adult, the surgeon came out of the operating room and told my family, "I don't know how she walked on that knee." As damaged and painful as it was, my knee never stopped working completely. It never let me down.

Then I began to think about the anterior cruciate ligament (ACL) I received in 2010, that was literally a gift from God. The ACL attaches the thigh bone to the shin bone and stabilizes the knee along with other ligaments in the knee. I often speak of ACL reconstruction surgery because that surgery was the most difficult in terms of pain and recovery time but what most don't know is that my ACL came from donated tissue from an organ donor. I am a transplant recipient. We often think of heart, liver and lung transplant as the only kind of transplants. But donors also designate other tissue as well. Donated tissue for transplant changes lives. It changed mine.

I remember the day I left the hospital after ACL surgery. The nurse handed me my donor papers so that I could write the family of my donor a thank you letter. I still tear up when I think about it. Having the tissue, the essence and the spirit of another human inside of you is a powerful, awe-inspiring feeling. Words are not enough to express my thanks for the gift I was given.

Before I knew it, I began to sob uncontrollably. I realized that to get a new knee and move forward, I must first part with the old knee. Total knee replacement surgery removes the entire knee, along with the ACL. Total knee replacement would remove my damaged joint but it also meant that my precious gift is removed too. I cried as I thought about giving up a part of me.

However, I knew that the surgery was part of God's plan for me. It was part of my journey in life. It was part of my purpose in life. So the next step I took was saying good-bye to part of me. As difficult as it was, I knew it was time for me to move to the next phase of my journey.

I lovingly parted with my knee joint and my ACL.

Another aspect of psychological preparation is letting your pride down. Go ahead, lay it down. We as a society are so independent. Most of us take on this super hero persona proudly. We juggle 10,000 things at once and feel a great sense of pride in our ability to do so. We act as if we don't need anyone for anything.

I hate to break the news to you, you will need assistance from others after TKR. You need assistance from your family and in my case, from friends. My family does not live in the same city so it took a well-coordinated effort to make sure I had someone at home with me the first week.

After the first few days, I managed by having someone stop by every evening. Caring for myself all day was exhausting but I managed. In the end, I believe it made me stronger and I recovered more quickly because no one waited on me hand and foot.

Don't panic, you are typically able to go to the toilet alone but you need help getting in and out of bed the first few days, showering, preparing meals, and household tasks. Plus, you are not able to drive the first two weeks regardless of which leg it is. If it is your driving leg it might take longer. Surgery greatly reduces your reaction time. Moving from the gas to the brake quickly is simply not going to happen. Drive before you are ready and you are a danger to yourself and everyone else on the road.

You take powerful narcotics for pain after surgery. You cannot drive while taking narcotics. That is called driving under the influence (DUI). It is illegal!

Kimberly Dixon, M.Ed., CPC, CCRC

CHAPTER FOUR
WHAT DO I NEED?

The afterthought is good, but forethought is better.
- Norwegian Proverb

Part of preparing for surgery is making sure you have everything you need once you are released from the hospital.

The list of items needed includes:

1. Pain medication. Pick up pain medication from the hospital pharmacy or on the way home. Do not go home expecting to pick it up later. By the time you check out from the hospital, get in the car and ride home, you will NEED it. I learned from experience to never, ever leave the hospital without your pain medication.

After outpatient ACL reconstruction surgery in 2010, I learned my lesson. I felt good when I left the hospital because I had a nerve block. My leg had no feeling. However, by the time I got home I was in serious pain. The nerve block wore off quickly. The pain was so severe that I felt I would surely go crazy. I wanted to literally pull my hair out. The pharmacy nearest my house did not have the medication prescribed for me. My sister went to another pharmacy to get it. It was only a few extra miles but I thought I would lose my mind from the pain in that short time period. Take my advice to get your pain medication before you leave the hospital. Every hospital has a pharmacy on site. Also if you know from previous experience that pain medication makes you nauseous, inform your doctor. He or she can prescribe a different pain medication or a medication for nausea.

2. Comfortable loungewear or pajamas. After surgery you are not restricted to bed, however you spend considerable time napping the first few days at home due to pain medication. If you are asleep, you might as well be comfortable. Expect some swelling, so

try to avoid tight or close-fitting clothes. Ladies yoga pants are cute and comfortable under most circumstances but they feel like sausage casing on a swollen leg so I find from my own experiences that it is best to wear loose fitting pants until the swelling subsides.

Comfortable, non-binding clothes are needed for physical therapy (PT). Do not wear jeans to PT. Even loose fitting jeans, are too restrictive for knee PT. Some physical therapists prefer the patient to actually wear shorts. Shorts allow them to see the joint and the muscles activate. If you wear pants, make sure they are loose enough to roll up past your knee.

3. Good shoes for walking. Most doctors recommend beginning a daily walking routine soon after surgery. Although it will be painful in the beginning, moving your new joint is actually the best thing for it. Walking helps the joint to regain function and flexibility and builds muscle strength. A muscle loses strength as a result of surgery and swelling. Walking will help strengthen the muscle. You walk every day and gradually increase the distance. A good supportive shoe takes stress off your knees, hips and back.

It is highly likely that you will need new shoes for after surgery. Bowed-legs, knock knees and other knee issues cause uneven wear of shoes. My shoes were famous for leaning to the side. Be safe, get some new shoes! Besides, I found that after surgery my old shoes were downright uncomfortable.

4. If you already own a walker or cane, great. If you do not own any mobility aids, do not worry about them before the surgery. A hospital case worker or occupational therapist typically visits you prior to leaving the hospital to ensure that you have the mobility aids you need to navigate safely once you are home. If you do not receive a visit from anyone concerning mobility aids, simply ask your nurse how to procure those items.

Getting the items you need before your hospital stay makes the process much simpler and easier.

Surgery Checklist

Pre-Admission Testing Date: _____

Surgery Date: _____

Hospital: _____

Surgeon: _____

Arrival Time: _____

Surgery Time: _____

Important Contacts' Phone Numbers

_____

_____

_____

- o File Disability Claim (FMLA)
- o Inform Employer of Leave of Absence
- o Verify Hospital Pre-authorization
- o Call creditors (mortgage, credit cards, student loan, etc.) to verify disability coverage or ask for forbearance
- o Make Follow-up calls if the above requires it
- o Attend pre-admission testing
- o Attend pre-admission classes (if required)
- o Lounge wear
- o Shoes
- o Other _____
- o _____
- o _____
- o _____
- o _____

CHAPTER FIVE
THE SURGERY

In nothing be anxious, but in everything, by prayer and petition with thanksgiving, let your requests be made known to God.
- Philippians 4:6

Today is the day you take the big step towards a new life. Everything starts now.

The morning of surgery is scary for most and a little unnerving. You can do this. You have everything you need inside of you to overcome the obstacles recovery brings. You waited long enough to have the life you desire. Today you stand at the threshold of getting what you want.

To get what you want, you must know what you want.

What do you want? Why do you want it?

It is of upmost importance to know your big "why." Why are you doing this?

The goal for many is to regain function and experience less pain, but why do you want this?

Do you want to play with your kids or grandkids? Do you want to start a new hobby? Do you want to travel more?

As a child, I loved roaming through the woods with my siblings. I never lost my love of being outside. Slowly I lost my ability to walk outside. My right knee barely bent, so walking through the woods was impossible. Walking at all was a challenge. From 2011 to 2015, I used a cane and I wore a brace on my right leg. Walking was painful even with my mobility aids. Walking a quarter of a mile was difficult, and walking through the woods was impossible.

I wasn't steady on my feet so walking on uneven surfaces was challenging. I couldn't bend my knee enough to step over most things. And quite frankly, I didn't trust myself enough to venture into the woods alone. Being in the woods is a beautiful, centering experience to me, but the woods are also home to animals and pose dangers you don't encounter on a day-to-day basis. I felt it best for me to stay out of the woods in my condition.

My "why" for getting my knees replaced was and still is being able to hike through the woods again. As a matter of fact, I now plan to hike in all 50 states. I am like Forest Grump, once I start walking I am not going to stop. I want to walk everywhere I can. I remember sitting on the couch crying because I wanted to go outside. It was my desire to go outside that started the crying, screaming match with God.

The big "why" is your motivation. The motivation behind the goal encourages you when you feel discouraged, are in pain or you are frustrated. You experience all of these emotions after surgery. Sometimes all within the same hour.

My desire to hike in all 50 states keeps me going. It keeps me motivated when I don't want to do PT. It keeps me motivated when I am in pain. It keeps me motivated when I feel frustrated at the slow progress.

What is your big "why?" What is your motivation?

Take a moment to record your answers.

What do you want?

_____

_____

_____

_____

_____

_____

_____

_____

_____

_____

Why do you want it? Be as detailed as possible. More details makes your motivation stronger. The stronger your motivation, the better the outcome.

_____

_____

_____

_____

_____

_____

_____

_____

_____

_____

_____

_____

_____

What are you willing to do to get your desired outcome?

_____

_____

_____

_____

_____

What obstacles do you foresee?

_____

_____

_____

_____

_____

_____

How will you overcome obstacles?

_____

_____

_____

_____

_____

_____

Three tools I use to overcome obstacles are prayer, meditation and music. Prayer helps me remember that I am not alone and that I have a place I can go when I need a refuge. Meditation helps me re-center myself. The deep breathing helps me regain clarity. It's hard to think clearly when you are in pain. Meditation helps me gain a clearer perspective. I love music. Music makes me happy. I have several songs as my go-to songs for inspiration and motivation. I call them my personal anthems. They come from all genres and they all make me want to stand up, sing, dance and do my PT. Find tools that work for you and use them.

Answering these question before your surgery will help you stay focused when you feel frustrated, sad, and plain "ole" tired. Total knee replacement is major surgery and the recovery is difficult. However you must stay in the game. Staying in the game requires you to forge ahead when you don't feel like it.

One last note: prior to your surgery you are scheduled for a pre-operative visit. Typically, it is scheduled in the 2 weeks prior to surgery. The pre-op visit entails a visit with your surgeon to go over the details and a visit with the anesthesia team. This visit takes several hours so plan, accordingly.

The anesthesia team goes over your medical history in detail, draws blood, does a EKG and provides other instructions such as showering before the surgery with a specific type of soap. During the pre-op visit, the nurse tells you not to eat or drink ANYTHING after midnight the day before your surgery. Please follow these instructions.

In other words, do not stop for your favorite coffee on the way to the hospital.

Do not take a bite of that bagel or have eggs.

A spoonful or a bite is still food and coffee is a drink.

I know this sounds facetious but the surgeon will absolutely cancel your surgery if you ate or drank anything.

Do Not wear any deodorant, powders, perfume, cologne, make-up or body sprays. During surgery many electrodes are attached to your body to monitor your vital signs while you are under anesthesia. These products cause the electrodes to not stick properly and come off during surgery.

Good luck with your surgery and recovery!

Remember, YOU are great and capable of great things!

SOURCES

Ancient Proverbs:
http://www.worldofproverbs.com/2012/05/public-domain-published-before-1923.html

Cover Image: Painfull (sic) knee

Credit line © Sebastian Kaulitzki | Dreamstime.com

Cover Design: Kassand Graphic Design

Image: Knee Joint Labeled Diagram

Credit line © Rob3000 | Dreamstime.com

Image: Stages of knee Osteoarthritis (OA)

Credit Line © Designua | Dreamstime.com

Kimberly Dixon, M.Ed., CPC, CCRC

ADDITIONAL RESOURCES

For more on FMLA visit: http://www.dol.gov/whd/fmla/

Blog on arthritis and mental, physical and spiritual well-being: www.bowlegsandarthritis.com

See videos of my hospital stay and recovery process. YouTube channel:
https://www.youtube.com/channel/UCRiB9_be_VmI1s20CoZqZAg

Looking for a life coach to help your deal with chronic pain? Visit www.joyfullivingwithkimberlydixon.com

Look for more books in the Now What? series:

I Have Arthritis, Now What?

I Had a Knee Replacement, Now What? (Coming soon)

Kimberly Dixon, M.Ed., CPC, CCRC

REVIEWS

Kimberly fills in the gap from Health Professional to Patient. She has carved out a niche that will give ease to the patient who has to decide and go through the process of knee replacement. Powerful firsthand experience and a life testimony that will help anyone with chronic pain!

> Rev. Angel Onley-Livingston, NBCC, LPC
> House of Abba Family Outreach Center LLC
> Author of *Healing While Grieving*

A friend gave me Kimberly Dixon's *I Need a Knee Replacement, Now What?* just as I'd started thinking I needed a knee replacement, but didn't have the first idea where to start. This book gave me the frame of reference I needed to think about it and make a plan. I'm very thankful for the excellent information, shared experiences, and faith-based approach!

> Louisa W. (prospective knee
> replacement recipient)
> Mystic, CT

Great book! I found it to be very informative and useful. The advice you give is absolutely crucial in every phase of surgery, including pre and post-surgery. I missed some of the steps that I should've taken for my knee replacement surgery. This guide would have benefited me greatly. I especially liked the financial planning section and support system setup for after surgery. It's extremely difficult immediately after surgery and up to a week or so. This is a must-have for those facing knee replacement surgery.

> Malcolm D. (knee replacement recipient)
> Winston-Salem, NC

Kimberly's thought provoking, straightforward; approach to a total knee replacement is both nail-biting and invigorating. I'm grateful that Kimberly has chosen to share her life changing experience.

Her courage, strength, and positive attitude will change the lives of others.

Kyre Ward Osei (caregiver of TKR recipient)
Woodbridge, VA

ABOUT THE AUTHOR

Kimberly Dixon, M.Ed., CPC, CRCC holds a master's degree in education in which her focus was psychology. She is a certified professional coach, a certified Christian coach and a neuro-linguistic programming practitioner. In addition, she is a blogger and a speaker.

In her life, she had 8 surgeries on her legs and knees. Each surgery was different from the other in regards to recovery time, physical therapy, and pain level. The one thing they all had in common was that they all taught her something different. The daily struggles, surgeries and pain endured taught her many valuable lessons about life, health, happiness and perseverance. The purpose of the *Now What* series and blog is to share her experiences with others and perhaps helps someone else experiencing a similar situation. Her coaching practice although open to all specializes in coaching people with chronic pain or chronic illnesses.

53620002R00033

Made in the USA
Charleston, SC
12 March 2016